With Joy
and BEST WISHES
TO DAVID
MAY YOUR PATH OF DISCOVERY
and JOURNEY of the HEART
BE ETERNALLY Filled with
HAPPINESS and PEACE —— !
in the Spirit of the Arts
M. Kerstead-Houston

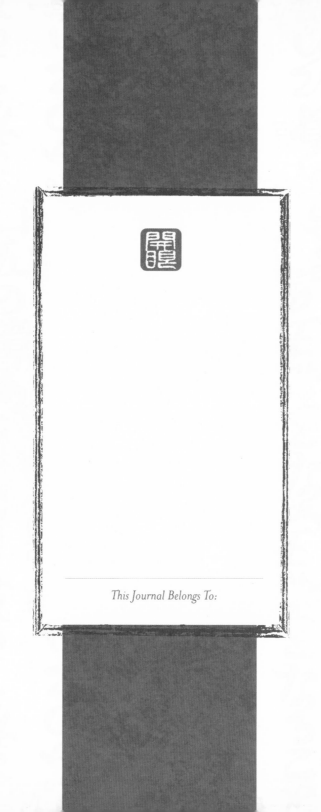

This Journal Belongs To:

THE FIVE AWARENESSES

WE ARE *aware* THAT ALL GENERATIONS
OF OUR ANCESTORS AND ALL FUTURE
GENERATIONS ARE *present* IN US.

WE ARE AWARE OF THE *expectations* THAT
OUR ANCESTORS, OUR *children*
AND THEIR CHILDREN HAVE OF US.

WE ARE AWARE THAT OUR JOY, PEACE,
freedom AND HARMONY ARE THE JOY, *peace,*
FREEDOM AND *harmony* OF OUR ANCESTORS,
OUR CHILDREN AND THEIR CHILDREN.

WE ARE AWARE THAT *understanding*
IS THE VERY *foundation* OF LOVE.

WE ARE *aware* THAT BLAMING AND ARGUING
NEVER HELP US AND ONLY *create* A WIDER GAP
BETWEEN US, THAT ONLY *understanding,* TRUST
AND LOVE CAN *help* US CHANGE AND *grow.*

Birth AND *Death*

ARE ONLY DOORS

THROUGH WHICH

WE MUST PASS,

sacred

THRESHOLDS

ON OUR *journey.*

When we live in AWARENESS,
it is easy to see MIRACLES everywhere.

IN

OUT

Deep Slow

CALM

Peace

SMILE

RELEASE

Present Moment

WONDERFUL

Moment

WHEN

we

FEEL

happy

and

peaceful,

our

HAPPINESS

and

peace

RADIATE

around

us,

and others

can

ENJOY

it

as

well.

When we ENTER *the present* MOMENT *deeply, our* REGRETS *and sorrows* DISAPPEAR...

we DISCOVER *life with all its* WONDERS…

ASK *yourself, What am I* WAITING *for to make me* HAPPY?

Why am I not HAPPY *right now?*

BREATHING IN, *I am a mountain,*

Imperturbable, Still, ALIVE, *Rigorous,*

BREATHING,

out,

I

FEEL

solid

The

WAVES

of

EMOTION

Can

never

CARRY

me

AWAY.

A teacher cannot GIVE *you the* TRUTH. *The truth is already in* YOU.

You only need to open YOURSELF *body, mind and heart.*

RECOGNIZE *your deep* DESIRE…

TO LIVE *in* PEACE *and safety, to have the* SUPPORT *you need, and to* PRACTICE MINDFULNESS.

Practicing MINDFULNESS *helps us learn to* APPRECIATE *the* WELL-BEING *that is already there.*

With MINDFULNESS, *we* TREASURE *our* HAPPINESS *and can* MAKE *it last longer.*

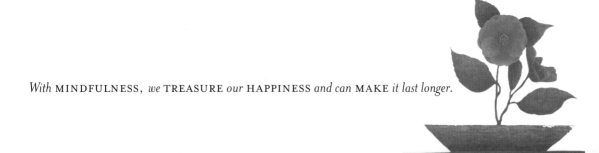

ENJOY *your* HAPPINESS *and* OFFER *it to everyone.*

Please make YOURSELF *into* SOMEONE *we can* RELY *on.*

What is most IMPORTANT is to FIND PEACE and to SHARE it with others.

True LOVE

contains respect.

We HAVE *more* POSSIBILITIES *available*

in EACH *moment than we* REALIZE.

There is NOTHING *to stop* YOU *from being in* TOUCH *with* LIFE *in the present* MOMENT.

The question is, do you have the EYES *that can* SEE *the sunset,* FEET *that can* TOUCH *the earth?*

I have ARRIVED *I am* HOME *In the* HERE, *In the the* NOW.

I am SOLID. *I am* FREE. *In the* ULTIMATE *I* DWELL.

THE TEARS *I shed* YESTERDAY *have become* RAIN.

May I LEARN *to look at* MYSELF *with the* EYES *of* UNDERSTANDING *and* LOVE.

In daily LIFE, *there is so* MUCH *to do and so little* TIME.
You may feel PRESSURED *to run all the time.* JUST STOP!

TOUCH *the ground of the present* MOMENT *deeply and you will touch* PEACE *and* JOY.

Each MOMENT *is a chance for us to make* PEACE *with the* WORLD, *to make peace*

POSSIBLE *for the* WORLD, *to make* HAPPINESS *possible for the* WORLD.

All the ELEMENTS

for your happiness

are ALREADY *here.*

EACH *moment*

you are ALIVE

IS A GEM,

SHINING *through*

and CONTAINING

EARTH *and sky*

and CLOUDS.

Practice LOOKING *deeply.*

You will SEE *the* CONDITIONS

that have CAUSED *you to be*

the WAY *you* ARE.

ACCEPT *yourself — your suffering and your* HAPPINESS *at the same time.*

To LOVE *is first of all to* ACCEPT *yourself as you actually* ARE.

FOLLOW *your breathing,*

DWELL *mindfully on your steps,*

and soon you will FIND

your BALANCE.

MAKE *each* MOMENT *an* OCCASION *to* LIVE *deeply,* HAPPILY, *in* PEACE.

If you are CAPABLE *of living deeply*

one MOMENT *of your life,*

you can LEARN

to LIVE *the same way*

all the other MOMENTS

of your LIFE.

The way we SPEAK *and* LISTEN *can* OFFER

others joy, HAPPINESS, *self-confidence,*

HOPE, *trust and* ENLIGHTENMENT.

KNOWING *that words can* CREATE *happiness or* SUFFERING

I am DETERMINED *to speak* TRUTHFULLY,

with words that INSPIRE *self–confidence,*

JOY, *and* HOPE.

A smile REFRESHES *your* WHOLE *being and* STRENGTHENS *your* PRACTICE.

Don't be AFRAID *to* SMILE.

May everyone be HAPPY *and* SAFE,

and MAY *their* HEARTS

be FILLED *with* JOY.

The Buddha

If you can MAKE *one* PEACEFUL *step,*

then PEACE *is* POSSIBLE.

Artwork
Richard Kirsten-Daiensai
Nicholas Kirsten-Honshin

Writing and Translations
Thich Nhat Hanh

Book Design
Stephanie Haller